CRANACH

PHAIDON

I. LUCAS CRANACH AT THE AGE OF 77 YEARS. 1550. Florence, Uffizi

CRANACH

BY E·RUHMER

WITH FIFTY PLATES IN FULL COLOUR

PUBLISHED BY THE PHAIDON PRESS

TRANSLATED FROM THE GERMAN
BY JOAN SPENCER

PRINTED IN GREAT BRITAIN
BY HUNT BARNARD & CO · LTD · AYLESBURY · BUCKS

LUCAS CRANACH THE ELDER

IT is to the generation born about 1470 that the visual arts in Germany owe such a wealth of creative talent – artists who, regarded as a whole, combine bold innovation with the simultaneous awareness that they have attained the peak, and thus temporarily the end, of their development. In this the German masters corresponded exactly with the Italians, whose general stylistic development had, however, progressed further: Florentine, Lombard or Venetian contemporaries of Cranach like Mariotto Albertinelli, Fra Bartolommeo, Bernardino Luini, Sodoma, Giorgione, Dosso Dossi, but particularly Michelangelo and Titian (assuming he really was born only five years after Cranach) stand in an exactly similar relation to the artists of the preceding generation. One thing is clear: the level of attainment reached by the Germans was precisely that reached by Mantegna, Bellini, Pollaiuolo, at most Signorelli and Botticelli – a level of art which already belonged to Italy's past. Though it is certain that the masters of the North exerted a considerable influence on the younger Italian mannerists they never attained the classic maturity of Giorgione or Titian.

Of all the outstanding German masters born about 1470 Lucas Cranach possessed this gift of classicism least. Stylistically he seems to stand outside his period, in fact he used to be regarded as capriciously retrograde and traditionalist, a belated Gothic, such was the extraordinary modernity of his approach and much of his subject matter. In actual fact Cranach was hardly a Gothic artist but such a sharply individual stylist that he could well be called a mannerist, not as following a general 'trend' but as possessing a completely independent originality. It is above all his attentive awareness of the spirit of his time, his intuitive grasp of contemporary spiritual reality, which ranks Cranach, with all his artistic failings and imperfections, with painters like Burgkmair, Mathias Grünewald and the rather younger artists like Hans Baldung Grien, Albrecht Altdorfer and Hans Holbein, thanks to whom German painting takes its place in the general humanist revival and in the Renaissance in Europe – literally at the last moment.

The fact that innovation was somewhat delayed and was accomplished not without precipitation, violence and eclecticism lends to this brief, somewhat hectic flowering the fascination of the eccentric and the intriguingly precarious. The flat plain style of late Gothic art – full of ideas and expression but stiff and often formless – held for the German of the 15th and even the early 16th century an irresistible and enduring attraction. Not for about a century after Donatello's early Florentine masterpieces and Masaccio's monumental paintings in the Cappella Brancacci was there any question of a genuine infiltration of the Renaissance into Germany.

The year of Cranach's birth, 1472, emerges with a pleasing certainty from two sources: a Latin commemorative piece by Matthäus Gunderam and the inscription on the artist's tombstone in the graveyard of St. Jacob's Church at Weimar. The actual family name is not quite certain; it is often said to be Sunder or Sonder. Cranach's father Hans styled himself 'Mahler' which is to be taken as an indication of his calling; he was not a miller, as is often claimed in the literature of the day, but a painter. It is futile to wonder whether he painted walls, was an interior decorator, or actually painted pictures, for in those days a man who did the one did the other. One can hardly assume that Cranach's father was a remarkable painter, for a Frankish–Saxon frontier town as small and insignificant as the artist's birthplace Kronach in the Frankenwald had certainly no artistic life of its own. Even so Friedländer (on p. 4 of his corpus of Cranach's paintings) reproduces a statue of John the Baptist dating from 1498 which is set into the porch of Kronach parish church and which is not only a significant work of art but is a striking anticipation of Cranach's later manner. It displays that specific 'curly style' which we shall later attempt to examine more closely. The Frankish element in Cranach's character and art is not particularly evident, much less so than the Eastern element. In the early middle ages Kronach did in fact suffer a strong Slav immigration and again in 1057 belonged temporarily to Moravia. In 1260 the little town was incorporated with the bishopric of Bamberg, to which it belonged until secularisation. Even today Kronach possesses charming medieval corners and impressive buildings, of which the mighty mountain fortress of Rosenberg is the most imposing.

Cranach, who spent most of his life in Wittenberg on the Elbe, a town set in a plain landscape, flat to the point of desolation, always endowed his pictures with the most romantic scenery and background landscapes: valleys, woods and hills, with towering crags surmounted by castles. Flat country has always been a fertile source of the ideal and the romantic in landscape painting: with Cranach the imagination of the plain-dweller was constantly nourished and enriched not only by specific fresh impressions of travel but also by old memories of the hills and woods near the little towns and castles of his native Frankenwald.

The artist took the name Cranach from his place of birth, Kronach. With the intellectual humour typical of the Wittenberg humanist circle the artist once allowed himself the amusement of improving on this adopted name and signed his Torgau altarpiece of 1509 (now in Frankfurt; Plate II) with the slightly latinised version 'Lucas Chronus'. Cranach's playful identification with the god of time can be variously understood: as a claim to more than local, if not international, importance or as an expression of his unusually rapid rate of work so highly praised by his contemporaries.

Matthäus Gunderam, whom we mentioned above, also a native of Kronach, tells us in his memoir (which was discovered in one of the knobs on the steeple of Wittenberg church) that Cranach was introduced to 'artem graphicam' by his father Hans Mahler. Between 1495 and 1498 Lucas, who in the earliest records also bears the name 'Maler', undertook work in his native Kronach for the neighbouring town of Coburg and also for Gotha further afield.

For the little town on the outermost periphery of Franconia the capital Nuremberg was the natural artistic centre. Whether or not Cranach's artistic and cultural development included one or several visits to the town before 1495, whether he is in fact a product of the Nuremberg Late Gothic school of painting, as would seem obvious, does not emerge from the early works extant, dating from soon after 1500, or from Cranach's vast output over the next half-century. What is quite clear is Cranach's debt to the Nuremberg Early Renaissance, i.e. to Albrecht Dürer who was only one year his senior but had developed earlier. But such an influence really proves nothing because it proceeds from models readily available to all and widely used. The main reason against alleging an unequivocal connexion between the apparently 'Gothic' Cranach and the Nuremberg Late Gothic is the fact that Cranach, so strikingly intent upon order after his move to Wittenberg, was in reality one of the most sovereign individualists in the German art of his time, more independent even than Dürer, almost as independent as Mathias Grünewald. All things considered it would seem best to leave open the question of Cranach's 'teacher'. His style is based on none of the celebrated masters: the natural influences he absorbed and made use of were always confined to motif. Cranach's influence is greater than his debt.

Not until 1500 or so does Cranach, now almost thirty, emerge as a valid artistic figure, geographically far removed from his starting point, namely in Vienna. There is abundant evidence of this Viennese period. Cranach himself is said to have told Melanchthon (at an unspecified date) that 'at an age of thirty-two . . . he lay very ill in Vienna in Austria'. And Scheurl mentions this stay in Vienna in a letter of 1509: 'Once, in Austria, you painted some bunches of grapes on a table so realistically that as soon as you left a magpie flew in and, as if annoyed at the deception, destroyed your newly completed work with its beak and claws'. Cranach's travels took him to Regensburg, then probably to Passau and Linz. In 1502, 1503 and 1504 Cranach was almost certainly in Vienna, where, as is clear from four of his most impressive portraits, he was in touch with two important university professors, the historian Johannes Cuspinian, also a native of Franconia, and the lawyer Stephan Reuss, a native of Constance who was elected to the rectorship of the University of Vienna a year after Cranach painted his portrait. Cranach made woodcuts for a Viennese printer and he painted among other things a *Crucifixion* which has been preserved down the centuries in the Schottenstift at Vienna (fig. 3). Also a *St. Jerome Penitent* of 1502, in Vienna (Plate 3), together with a number of other works listed by Friedländer, date with tolerable certainty from this period and were painted in Austria.

The most important examples of Cranach's earliest known style, apart from these four portraits, are the *Christ on the Cross* of 1503 in Munich (Plate 6) and the *Rest on the Flight to Egypt* of 1504 in Berlin (Plate 7). Together with the *Crucifixion* in the Schottenstift, two almost barbarically expressive altar wings in the Vienna Academy (see Plate 2), these paintings display in its purest form a stylistic tendency which we must now examine in some detail.

It is the style of the so-called Danube School, which must undoubtedly rank among its masterpieces Cranach's early paintings mentioned above. Even today the problem of the Danube School has not yet been finally solved. Its highly distinctive style is to be found in Regensburg and Passau on the Danube, in the work of Albrecht Altdorfer and Wolf Huber, but also in Switzerland in Nikolaus Manuel Deutsch, Urs Graf, Hans Leu the Younger, and in Austria in the Master of Mühldorf, Hans Pruckendorfer, Gordian Guckh, and Jörg Breu of Augsburg who worked there until 1502 and whose starkly expressive art is often seen, not without justification, as a decisive source of inspiration for Cranach's Austrian style. Breu's 'Zwettl altarpiece' dates from the same year, 1500, to which art historians assign the inception of one of Cranach's works such as the *Crucifixion* in the Vienna Schottenstift (fig. 3). This style spreads far to the north, even to the German sculpture of the period, as in the circle of the great Landshut woodcarver Hans Leinberger and of the eccentric Master H. L. of the upper Rhine and elsewhere. It is a style that springs from the Late Gothic but is entirely fresh, anticipating slightly the spread of the Italian Renaissance to Germany but then flourishing alongside it in its own right until about the middle of the sixteenth century. It is probably the specifically German interpretation of the humanist conception of 'intellectual freedom' in art.

It is less in the territory of the Upper Danube than in the northern half of the Duchy of Bavaria (Regensburg, Landshut), and the bishopric of Passau that this style seems to have originated and it is for this reason sometimes called the 'Bavarian style'. But when one reflects that the main achievement of this school, landscape painting, takes for its central theme the romantic scenery of the Upper Danube with its rocks, woods and streams, one prefers to retain the incorrect but colourful term 'Danube School', which is in current use.

Now the curious thing is that Cranach, so far as can be objectively ascertained from existing records, did not passively undergo the influence of a style long practised and firmly established locally on the banks of the Danube. Things must have happened differently because Cranach, the outsider, evolves the genuine, fully developed 'Danube Style' not only rather earlier than the more conservative Jörg Breu but in particular earlier than the celebrated local painters. The chief exponent of this type of landscape painting and this particular style, Albrecht Altdorfer, who was younger than Cranach, certainly does not emerge as a painter before 1505, though his earliest works are painted in the fully developed Danube style. It can certainly not be assumed that Cranach brought with him to the region this stylistic trend, which assumed such vital importance for German art: rather is it a natural consequence of the local stylistic tradition, which consistently displays the most direct preconditions for its birth and development. But it was left to the newcomer, with his unspoiled vision and an outsider's irreverent approach, to grasp the essential fascination of this style, to hasten its development with enthusiasm and to bring it to immediate perfection.

The Danube style is strongly picturesque, with an irresistible urge to manual virtuosity matched by a serious, genuinely artistic endeavour to capture the fleeting, shifting, relative quality of all phenomena by adequate artistic means. This called for a rapid, impressionistic method and the application of colour in contrasting ways (thick and thin). But this technique was but the painter's 'handwriting' through which he expressed his personality, in which he set down his character, his feelings and especially his emotions directly and without comment. This, in German art, was a completely new way for the most subjective self-revelation in painting. This may well be the specifically German parallel to the pure pictorial style of the Italian contemporaries of Cranach and Altdorfer, namely Giorgione and Titian. Cranach's artistic 'signature' is never so marked or so unequivocal in any of his other periods known to us as in this earliest one. The future Wittenberg court-painter gradually turned from this vehement and egocentric manner and submitted to the discipline of objectivity imposed upon him by his official activities for court and church and particularly for the Reformation, so that his style grew increasingly simpler, bolder and more abstract. But the curly line so characteristic of Cranach's Viennese period (and of the Danube style) is still retained, a curious linear ornamentation reminiscent at first of eddying, foaming water, then coming increasingly to resemble a network of veins, then finally hardening into a complex of gnarled roots. This curly style, this 'wavy serpentine line' with a singular formal relation to Cranach's heraldic beast, the winged snake, with which he signed his pictures from 1508 onwards, occurs everywhere except in the splendidly free, grandiose and realistic sketches in body-colour on paper for portraits (in Reims, Paris and Vienna; all of them recently attributed to Lucas Cranach the Younger). But in the official commissioned portrait involving the collaboration of workshop assistants this manner inevitably returns, particularly in the delineation of hair and draperies, and proves a more reliable means of identifying unsigned or unattested works by Cranach or his workshop than any signature. The decisive motif in the paintings of the Danube Style is landscape, which owes to the Danube School its preponderance in the picture as a whole and in fact its very existence as a pictorial category. This landscape art does not aim at topographical exactitude but at a usually dramatically heightened, romantic creation of mood. The landscape repertoire consists of peaceful valleys, sharply jutting crags and alpine ranges gleaming in the distance, softly rounded shrubs and pines ruffled by the wind. The pulsating rhythm implicit in the draughtsmanship and pervading every detail combines with the light effect in which near and far unite, to weld sky and water, light and shade, moist reflections, blustery wind, into a thrilling, vibrant unity.

In landscape painting the line always followed the impulse of the senses, the prompting of the hand, changing and bewitching everything; in figure painting this appears as expressive distortion or as mannered singularity. This is particularly true of Cranach's early drawings, of the way he animates, almost caricatures his figures in his attempt to model them and make them live. Not only do these tortured, lamenting, penitent figures display the ugliness of the living creature undergoing physical or spiritual torment: in his most exaggeratedly expressive distortions the young Cranach betrays with savage excess his own involvement. Of the masters of the Danube School neither Altdorfer nor Huber followed him far in this direction. The only possible resemblance is the work of the ecstatic woodcarver Hans Leinberger.

In view of these early works a future like Mathias Grünewald's might well have been prophesied for Cranach, and in fact Cranach's *Crucifixion* in Munich (Plate 6) can be compared with no other work but Grünewald's almost contemporary *Mocking of Christ* in the same museum. When Cranach strikes a softer, more idyllic note, as in the *Rest of the Holy Family* in Berlin (Plate 7), there is still no less tension. A great host of choiring angels and cherubs assures the required degree of excitement while the anguish of doubt in the expression of the ungainly Joseph hints at spiritual disturbance. The only equable figure is the Mother of Jesus: but the provocatively peasant quality of her attitude, the commonplace plainness of this touchingly charming, humble maiden contains far too much conscious characterization to be mere simple innocence. The lofty solemnity of the landscape with the tall weatherbeaten fir rising up in the centre of the picture completes the dramatic character of the scene.

A forced, highly exaggerated originality of composition is characteristic of the 'Danube Style' and is evident in Cranach's early work, particularly in the Munich *Crucifixion* of 1503. If I am not mistaken, Cranach was the first to have the bold idea, later copied by many others, of not showing the group of three crosses frontally and alongside each other, but of letting the spectator break in upon the scene from the side, where he sees one of the thieves from the back and Christ in profile; the prominent foreground is reserved, paradoxically enough, for the other thief (Plate 6). It is hard to decide whether Cranach was intent on revealing the Passion afresh in a more affecting, cruel and realistic light by means of the unusual angle at which he represents it, or whether his sole aim was to produce with greater virtuosity the impression of depth on a flat surface, thus proving his ability to paint a nude in the most difficult foreshortening. As in modern Expressionism two motives are almost inseparably interwoven: the purely artistic aim and the intellectual intention.

We have spoken of Cranach's great originality and have indicated that despite all the changes he introduced into the stylistic content of his pictures – some superficial, some (by 1505) very far-reaching – he nevertheless retained one constant feature both as draughtsman and painter, namely the 'hand-writing' which expressed his personality. This does not mean that he avoided every influence from other artists. Rosenberg points out that Cranach never copied another master closely – which is perhaps a rather sweeping statement. It is certainly clear that he gladly received stimuli from others and then showed his artistic independence in the freedom with which he interpreted and sometimes improved on his original. We have already referred to the importance of Dürer for Cranach. Even when still court painter at Wittenberg he was repeatedly confronted with Dürer in the works this great master of German art created for Cranach's patron, Duke Frederick the Wise. It should be observed by way of clarification that a relationship of mutual esteem must have existed between the two artists; Dürer drew Cranach's portrait when Cranach was staying with Frederick the Wise in Nuremberg (drawing in the Musée Bonnat, Bayonne). But after Dürer's death in 1528 Cranach appears to diverge more and more from the greater master.

So far as is known Cranach never went to Italy; but stimuli from Italian Renaissance art reached him in the most varied ways, sometimes still clear to us but usually no longer discernible. Art historians have seen many traces of Leonardo in Cranach. There is in fact an astonishing resemblance between certain caricatures of old men in the different versions of Cranach's *Christ with the Woman taken in Adultery* or in his popular scenes of *Old Lover and Young Woman* on the one hand and Leonardo's *Caricatures* on the other hand. Glaser mentions obvious connexions between Madonna and Pietà compositions by Cranach and similar works by Bellini; others assume Cranach to have been acquainted with the art of Mantegna and Pollaiuolo.

Cranach's female nudes (from 1509), usually standing erect before neutral dark backgrounds, are strikingly reminiscent of the same motif in Lorenzo Costa: the great single nudes in Budapest and Bologna. What could Cranach have known of Costa, when his own son Hans did not see Costa's work until 1537 in Bologna? Scheurl must have traced some kind of connexion to make him compare Cranach with Costa's Bolognese contemporary, Francesco Francia (to Cranach's advantage). Friedländer points to the really amazing similarity of pose between Giorgione's ideal Dresden *Venus* and Cranach's *Nymph of the Fountain,* a popular work existing in several variants. (Giorgione's picture did not reach Saxony before the end of the seventeenth century at the earliest.) (See Plates 33, 36 and 45.)

Cranach and Titian can be shown to have met in Augsburg, though not before 1550. The account books of the day actually mention a portrait of 'Thucia, the painter from Venice' by Cranach. Titian was then painting the portrait of Cranach's patron, the captive Elector Johann Frederick of Saxony.

It is natural enough for a German artist of Dürer's time to display Netherlandish influences, and they can in fact be traced in Cranach's style right to the end despite its considerable 'Gothic' element. Not only Venetian, but also Netherlandish art provides many probable models for the half-length composition so dear to Cranach. Swarzenski discerns Netherlandish characteristics in the Torgau altarpiece of 1509 which significantly also offers examples of *grisaille.* This is the more credible in that Frederick the Wise, who employed at his court a Netherlandish master called Jan (formerly identified with Mabuse), sent Cranach to the Netherlands for a few months late in 1508, perhaps on a commercial, perhaps on a diplomatic mission, but Scheurl alleges that the reason for the journey was the prince's wish to parade Cranach's 'talent'. It can be shown that Cranach was in Antwerp early in 1509. In Malines he was commissioned by the Emperor Maximilian to paint the portrait of the eight-year-old prince, the later Emperor Charles V.

Comparatively the most faithful copy by Cranach extant is the one he made, of similar dimensions (possibly in 1520), of Hieronymus Bosch's triptych on the *Last Judgement* (the original is in the Academy, Vienna; Cranach's copy in the Berlin Museum).

The importance Cranach and his circle always attached to Netherlandish art emerges from a report written by Cranach's son-in-law Dr. Brück in 1550 to the captive Elector in Augsburg which, as a tribute to the ageing painter's work, emphasises that it can bear comparison with that of Netherlandish painters.

So far we have treated Cranach's style entirely as an individual mode of artistic expression peculiar to himself. But after his move to Wittenberg in 1505 Cranach's work became year by year visibly less the achievement of one individual and was increasingly merged in the collective output of a workshop functioning almost mechanically; taking as its model Cranach's own personal style, reliably and certainly discernible only in the few drawings known to be from his hand and in the pre-Wittenberg pictures, the workshop applied it and disseminated it as a fruitful pattern.

II. THE HOLY KINSHIP. Centre panel of the so-called Torgau Altar-piece. 1509. Frankfurt, Staedel Institute

Fig. 1. *The Holy Kinship*. Vienna, Academy of Fine Arts

The activity of a workshop, too apt to be thought of as a specifically medieval phenomenon, appears nowhere in such breadth and fullness as in Cranach's which of course is post-medieval and functions right up to the threshold of the Baroque period. The medieval head of workshop does not normally emerge as an individual personality but remains an anonymous force. The output of the medieval workshop is governed by something quite different from a 'stylistic direction', something much more mechanical and at the same time intellectual, in no case an 'artist' in the sense current in Cranach's time. That is why the products of a medieval workshop are often stylistically dissimilar, diverging individually so far from the accepted norm that modern style criticism would, but for other independent evidence, fail to ascribe many a work to its correct source. The 'personal note' is almost obliterated.

But the workshop persists undiminished during the Renaissance and the Baroque period, though its composition and method of work undergo far-reaching changes. Here the dominant personality of the famous, socially pre-eminent master exerts supreme stylistic authority. The painter in question, whose specific manner is familiar to the art-loving public, commands a staff who execute his orders, imitate, cultivate and develop his style and even his 'handwriting'. The simple workshop master has developed into the 'artist-prince'. We know this to be true of Rubens and it is equally applicable to a painter like Cranach. He was the rich patrician raised to the rank of knight, the great civic authority and the creator and exponent of a highly popular style of painting in clamorous demand.

From the more or less anonymous workshop community two figures stand out: Cranach's painter sons Hans (died in 1537 in Bologna) and Lucas the Younger (born 1515 in Wittenberg, died 1586 in Weimar). Of Hans' output we know for certain very few works, and those are not very impressive. Lucas the Younger on the other hand appears in strong definition: undoubtedly less imaginative and less sensual than his father and extremely dependent on him stylistically, but nevertheless an artist of most elegant taste and considerable ability, with his own still more pronounced mannerist approach. The economy of means inherited from his father, the instinctive sureness of stylisation, the charm of the sentiments expressed, are all carried beyond his father's customary moderation and fall into well-bred affectation and bloodless artificiality.

Cranach the Elder always needed numerous assistants. A fascinating glimpse of his workshop is afforded by the 'Studies of Heads' to be found in Reims, the Louvre, London, Berlin, Vienna and various private collections. Standing technically midway between drawing and painting, most of these heads, with all the freshness of a sketch, certainly come from the hand of the elder Cranach, not the younger, and surpass in their formal dexterity and expressive penetration all his other known works. These *modelli* are indeed works of genius, some of the most astonishing achievements in the whole of German art. Even Dürer is far surpassed by the freedom and magnificence of form and technique seen in these portrait sketches (and in the animal studies in Paris, Montreal and Dresden), while their warmth and vitality far excel Holbein the Younger (Plates 25 and 48).

Here, then, we have the authentic patterns on which the workshop could draw at will when carrying out its commissions for portraits. They already contained a rich concentration of form and expression which enabled them to be reproduced under workshop conditions without loss of content.

It has been assumed that Cranach the Elder himself retired relatively early from participation in workshop activity and that the elder son Hans exerted a decisive influence on the style of the workshop until his death in 1537. The younger Lucas is then said to have taken over this function. There is, in view of the prolonged activity of Cranach the Elder until well beyond 1537, and of the meagre talent of his younger son, little foundation for the first assumption. As for the other view, the unity of the workshop productions is so great that it is quite impossible to tell whether the occasional stylistic changes that appear before the father's death are traceable to the son's originality or to a quite natural evolution towards stylistic maturity on the part of the father.

We also encounter artists who are clearly products of the Wittenberg workshop and who strive diligently to reproduce Cranach's style but also display unmistakable traces of their own individuality, not always an advantage. One of these was probably the painter of a picture dated 1516 which can be shown to have been done for Cardinal Albrecht, *The Martyrdom of S. Erasmus*, signed H+S (said to be Heinrich Vogtherr the Elder). The most prolific of these pupils of Cranach (as we may very well call them) is the painter called by Friedländer the 'Master of the Mass of St. Gregory' once alleged to be the pseudo-Grünewald then identified with Hans Cranach, but since Zülch recognised no doubt correctly as the Simon Franck who succeeded Grünewald as court painter to Cardinal Albrecht in Halle, then in Aschaffenburg, and to whom very many rather arid and heavy altar-paintings may be safely ascribed, the most extensive of which is the former high altar of the Marien-kirche in Halle of 1529 with the portrait of the Cardinal. Another painter who went to Cranach less to serve than to learn from him is Franz Tymmermann, who is known to have been sent in 1538 by the Hamburg council as apprentice to Cranach for a couple of years. Other renowned Middle German painters who were pupils of Cranach are the three Krodel brothers and Hans Brosamer (the monogrammist HB), certainly also the Swiss Gottfried Leigl, then Peter Roddelstedt, Georg Böhm, Johann Kreuter and others.

But the most illustrious witnesses to Cranach's artistic significance are painters of note who occasionally imitated him from a distance. In the case of the often cited Jacopo de' Barbari the connexion is not quite clear. It is certain that the Venetian, fresh from the atmosphere of Bellini, was certainly working in Wittenberg from 1503 to 1505 and underwent a radical Nordic transformation. He certainly came under Dürer's influence for a time. But works like the realistic still-life in the Munich Pinakothek, the graceful nude, *Galatea*, in Dresden or the portrait of Heinrich von Mecklenburg in the Hague are clearly reminiscent of Cranach. However, if it is remembered that the Italian painter worked in Wittenberg before the German, whose style immediately underwent a remarkable transformation, and that the Munich still-life dates also from before Cranach's arrival, that in fact the Cranach portraits which really bear comparison with the Mecklenburg painting of 1507 are of a slightly later date, one has doubts as to who was the innovator and who the borrower, Cranach or Jacopo de' Barbari.

There is on the other hand no doubt that one of the most powerful and individual of contemporary German painters, Hans Baldung Grien of Strassburg, also very active in Central Germany, chose Cranach as his guiding star on more than one occasion. This is most clearly seen in the *Portrait of a Lady*, 1530 (perhaps even copied from Cranach), in the Thyssen collection, in the Berlin *Caritas* and in more or less all of the female nudes he painted. Finally Baldung repeated several times as a wood-cut the engraved portrait of Luther which came from Cranach's workshop in 1520. But quite apart from these representative witnesses to the wide influence of Cranach's art, his style spread throughout Central Germany; sixteenth-century popular imitations of Cranach may still be found in many a Mid-German village church.

But to return to Cranach's Wittenberg workshop. The authentic signature of the workshop is, first, the master's monogram, then the snake symbol. From 1504–6 Cranach signed L.C. with the letters intertwined, sometimes in conjunction with the snake symbol which later he uses alone. Cranach uses this sign after a coat of arms is conferred on him early in 1508. It shows a snake with a crown on its head, a ring in its nose and (as they are called in the relevant document) bat's wings. Between 1515 and 1537 Cranach bears in his escutcheon only the snake symbol with the bat's wings upright. But about 1537, the year of Hans Cranach's death (an event formerly often mentioned in this connexion) the bat's wings become gently drooping bird's wings.

The snake symbol is a workshop label, the stamp of guarantee of Cranach's workshop, but it tells us nothing about the absolute authenticity of the picture bearing such a mark. Friedländer has observed that between 1505 and 1515 a particularly large number of works are unsigned. This may be mere chance or there may be natural external reasons: the signature may, for example, have been on the original frame (now lost), as was the case with Grünewald's altarpiece of *Our Lady of the Snows* at Aschaffenburg and many other works. After the death of Lucas Cranach the Elder in 1553 the younger son, who had been the real head of the Wittenberg workshop at least since his father's departure, adopted the same snake symbol as his coat of arms until his death. During this later period paintings in the Cranach manner often bear individual signatures like H.r., V., VT, VS and so on.

Cranach must have enjoyed considerable prestige already, when in 1504 the Elector Frederick the Wise of Saxony requested his services as court painter. In the spring of 1505 he complied with this request.

The small Saxon town of Wittenberg on the Elbe – 'on the frontiers of civilisation', as Cranach's friend Scheurl would say to describe its geographical and intellectual position – had already emerged somewhat from its insignificance. The Prince was not content merely to improve and adorn the castles in Wittenberg, Torgau, Lochau, Coburg and so on, and to enlarge and beautify his little capital, but in 1502 he also founded a university which, later linked with Halle to which town it moved, still flourishes today. The most famous of its teachers were the physician and theologian Polisch von Mellerstadt, the lawyer Christoph Scheurl (already mentioned several times as a friend of Dürer and Cranach), Hieronymus Schurff, the renowned professor of ecclesiastical law who stood by Luther at Worms and who married into Cranach's family, and above all Philipp Melanchthon.

The Prince's most successful efforts lay in the patronage of art. The Dutchman Jan (formerly often identified with Gossaert surnamed Mabuse), the Venetian Jacopo de' Barbari, a Master Kunz, a Master Ludwig, had already served the Prince as court painters before Cranach. Frederick commissioned work from the painters Michael Wolgemut and Hans Burgkmair, the sculptor Konrad Meit and the Nuremberg bronze founder Vischer. But Albrecht Dürer took pride of place. As early as 1496 he probably painted the young prince's portrait in an important tempera painting (now in the Berlin Museum). There is another portrait of the Prince dated 1524, that is a year before his death: it is the famous engraving B 104, undoubtedly based on a drawing made by Dürer when the Prince was visiting Nuremberg. Dürer also painted for Frederick the Wise the *Seven Sorrows of Mary* (Munich and Dresden), the triptych of the *Dresden Altar*, the *Adoration of the Magi* in the Uffizi and the *Martyrdom of the Ten Thousand* in Vienna. Much of Dürer's other work for Wittenberg has been lost. Thus it was by no means to a cultural desert that Cranach was summoned, to a place where he could do no other than shine. There was also for some years (until 1509) a second, older court painter working alongside him. Even so Cranach does seem to have enjoyed from the start an extraordinary renown: his salary of a hundred golden guilders was double that of his predecessors.

On 6th January 1508 the Prince honoured the new court painter by granting him a coat of arms.

15

Cranach's heraldic bearings were from now on the winged snake with which he immediately began to sign most of the products of his workshop. That Cranach put more than his artistic talent at the disposal of the court is repeatedly seen. This versatile, able, cordial and yet dependable Frank could obviously serve in many ways: the example of the Netherlands trip of 1508–9 has already been briefly mentioned.

Cranach, who was rapidly becoming prosperous, is first named in the Wittenberg register of taxes in 1510. From 1513 he paid dues on a house and landed property in Wittenberg, where he also kept a wine-shop. (He was liable for taxation in 1507 but for six years his taxes were expressly remitted). In 1518 we learn that the artist also owns a house in the Thuringian town of Gotha.

In 1519 the respected courtier and rich bourgeois was for the first time appointed treasurer to the Wittenberg town council. The following year the Prince granted him the privilege of apothecary which carried with it the magnificent apothecary's house in Wittenberg market at the corner of the Elbstrasse. Here the artist sold not only medicine and drugs but also, by royal privilege, fine colonial wares, spices and sweet wine.

In 1520 we read of a students' revolt which caused a considerable stir but was specially directed against Cranach and his workshop assistants. The background is not quite clear but the ostensible complaint was the granting of a coat of arms to the court painter and his assistants. Possibly this is nothing more than a testimony to the envy aroused by invidious social preference. According to another view the trouble was caused by Catholic machinations against the influential friend of Luther who protested against the disturbances but sought to make light of them.

Further evidence that Cranach was one of the most prominent citizens of Wittenberg is afforded by the fact that in 1523, when the painter was town councillor for the second time, the banished King Christian of Denmark took refuge in his house.

By 1524 Lucas Cranach owned a bookshop and, in collaboration with Döring, a fellow town councillor, ran a printing works combined with a paper mill. Apart from the sale of books, many of which were procured abroad, he sold Luther's writings and his own prints. In the course of this same year Cranach was involved in a legal dispute with the famous printer Melchior Lotter.

In May 1525 Frederick the Wise died. Cranach was commissioned by his brother John the Constant, who succeeded him, to submit plans for Frederick's tomb in the Schlosskirche. Together with his fellow councillor Döring the painter was assigned the task of distributing alms to the poor after the funeral.

In 1525–6, 1528–9 and 1531–2 Cranach was again a councillor. During John's reign which lasted only seven years the painter seems to have had less to do for the court. Instead, though still court painter, he was repeatedly commissioned by other patrons, of whom more will be said later – commissioned not only as a painter but (as in the case of Duke Albert of Prussia in Königsberg) as a book dealer.

Income tax figures for 1528 reveal that of all the inhabitants of Wittenberg, a town of barely four hundred houses, Cranach alone possessed four and in addition various landed properties. Together this represents a value of 4066 guilders, which makes Cranach the richest citizen of the town.

With John's successor, John Frederick the Magnanimous, Cranach formed even closer ties than with Frederick the Wise. In addition he climbed still further up the ladder of civic honours. After holding office as councillor from 1534–35 he was elected mayor in 1537 – an honour he retained alternately with a colleague until 1544. In the years when he was out of office he was again entrusted with the financial administration of the town.

In 1546 high politics intervened in the destinies of the country, the Prince and his court painter. The Emperor Charles V declared the heads of the so-called League of Schmalkalden under the ban of empire. The result was the outbreak of the Schmalkaldic War, which was to have an unfortunate issue for the evangelical princes and gravely endanger the Protestant cause. On 24 April 1547 the armies of the League were defeated at Mühlberg on the Elbe (Titian's famous equestrian portrait of Charles V, 1548, now in the Prado, shows the Emperor as the victor of Mühlberg), and John Frederick was taken prisoner. His court painter, Cranach, was summoned by the Emperor to his camp at Piesteritz where he was extremely honourably treated and is said to have saved his humiliated master's life. John Frederick begged Cranach through his son-in-law Dr. Christian Brück to follow him into captivity but Cranach, now seventy-five, at first refused on the grounds of his failing health. After the title of Elector of Saxony passed to Moritz of Saxony Cranach as art director and trusted friend of the deposed John Frederick supervised the removal from Wittenberg of countless art treasures, particularly those of the Schlosskirche (including Dürer's *Martyrdom of the Ten Thousand*).

Finally in 1550 the old man decided to visit his master in Augsburg to help him pass his time with 'sundry portrayals and other pictures'. After making his will and laying down all his offices Cranach left Wittenberg for ever. In Augsburg, as is clear from an account dated 1552, he resumed his activities as a painter on a considerable scale. We learn from a contemporary witness that the aged man still enjoyed the best of health both physically and intellectually and could not endure 'a single hour of idleness'. As has been mentioned he painted Titian's portrait during this Augsburg period. In 1551 Cranach went with the Prince to Innsbruck.

In 1552 John Frederick was reinstated as Duke. The new capital was Weimar, where Cranach also took up his residence. He lived and had his workshop in the house of the Chancellor Georg Brück, the father-in-law of his daughter Barbara who had died in the meantime.

On 16 October 1553 Lucas Cranach the Elder died at Weimar aged eighty-one and was buried in the St. Jacob's cemetery.

In connexion with Cranach's activities and significance as court painter to three Saxon princes of the Ernestine line mention may be made here of his other princely patrons who show how admirably the painter must have expressed the taste of the German aristocracy of his time, and how perfectly and graciously he fulfilled all his commitments. The Emperors Maximilian I and Charles V and the King of Denmark have already been mentioned, as have the Dukes Moritz of Saxony and Albert of Prussia. Even the Queen Mother of France acquired some of Cranach's pictures, given her by Frederick the Wise in exchange for relics.

Most of these works were portraits or altars. Of still greater interest perhaps is the honour implied in the request made by the Emperor Maximilian in 1515 that Cranach, together with Dürer, Hans Burgkmair, Jörg Breu, Albrecht Altdorfer, Hans Baldung Grien, and an unknown artist should provide marginal illustrations for the Emperor's famous prayerbook. Thus all the outstanding German painters of the day collaborated on a single project, all modelling their work directly on that of the leading artist, Albrecht Dürer. It is astonishing to see how contemporary judgment coincides with the verdict of modern art criticism.

Cranach's workshop in Wittenberg was not always called upon to produce ambitious panel pictures. Decorative painting and other occasional work of the most varied kind were all part of the everyday output. Of Cranach's murals in the castles of Wittenberg, Torgau, Lochau, Lichtenberg, Weimar, Wolfersdorf, Coburg, etc., nothing, alas, remains, though we do know that in these works

Cranach made use not only of fresco technique but also, in the Venetian manner, used canvas as his base. Sometimes Cranach undertook interior decoration as in the Wittenberg Town Hall, where in 1525 he not only painted pictures on the ceiling but also painted the doors, windows and walls. In allegorical work, in which he combined his special gifts, the local conditions and the wishes of his patrons, Cranach particularly excelled as a painter of animals. Thus in the shooting lodge at Lochau he painted partridges and ducks on the walls. As Cranach was a frequent guest on his master's hunting expeditions it fell to him to reproduce in watercolour each day's catch while still fresh. These animal studies, several of which are preserved (cf. Plate 48) may well have served as model for such murals (and also for some panel pictures). Cranach's animal paintings aroused general admiration and all kinds of stories (some founded on fact) were told about their realism, like the one from Vienna related above. 'In Coburg,' Scheurl goes on, 'you painted a stag. When strange dogs see this they bark at it.' And he continues, 'But what shall I say of a wild boar which our generous Prince sent the Emperor as a present, and whose image you contrived with such art that a hound on seeing it was so alarmed that its hair stood on end? In Torgau you painted on the walls hanging hares, pheasants, peacocks, partridges, ducks, quails, thrushes, wood pigeons and other birds of the same kind with such astounding realism that once the Count of Schwarzburg commanded the game to be removed to prevent a foul smell,' etc.

In 1513 the painter, with a team of ten assistants, was working in the castle of Torgau on the preparations for the wedding of Duke John of Saxony. He had to paint not only wall-hangings but also tabards and crests and above all a bridal couch, which was much admired and was adorned, as Philipp Engelbrecht relates in detail in his Latin epithalamium, 'with scenes from antiquity'. Four years later ceremonial sleighs for the court were decorated in Cranach's workshop. In 1521 the artist painted the organ-case of the Schlosskapelle in Weimar. For the tomb of Frederick the Wise in the Schlosskirche in Wittenburg, executed by Peter Vischer the Younger in 1525, Cranach provided models in wood and three drawings, with the intention of painting the completed cast in lifelike colours. The wedding of the Elector John Frederick, celebrated with great pomp on 1st July 1527 in Torgau, gave him a further opportunity to exercise his gift for occasional art.

In 1528 Cranach worked on the courtyard of the Wittenberg archers' guild; in 1535 he painted a summerhouse in Torgau. In 1542 he had to paint two thousand shields for the Saxon-Hessian armies engaged in the campaign against Duke Henry of Brunswick. He was required to decorate gun barrels, to design tapestries, to attend to court dress, and to design coins and medals. In view of the vast range and wealth of his output in the useful arts it is doubly astonishing that Cranach (with his workshop) is also one of those artists of whom we have the greatest number of paintings.

Amongst the larger paintings mention must first be made of the portraits, again chiefly admired by Cranach's contemporaries because of their realism . . . 'You paint people who seem alive and whom everyone recognises immediately at sight. . . . But you painted the virtuous Duke John so admirably that, not once but repeatedly, the people of Lochau, upon entering the castle and seeing through the window just the upper half of the picture, bared their heads and knelt to him as is their custom.'

The fidelity and naturalism of the mature Cranach's portraits is certainly not their only, perhaps not even their greatest, merit. Their distinction lies above all in an individual grandeur of style. This is true even though they were very often mass-produced in the workshop. Once Cranach was commissioned by John Frederick to produce immediately sixteen portraits of his ancestors and on another occasion 'sixty pairs of little panels' with portraits of Frederick the Wise and John the Constant.

If we regard as more or less by Cranach's hand only those portraits which come nearest to the Reims 'models' in the freshness of their conception, the power of their modelling and the conviction of their mimic expression, we can still perceive that Cranach's style of portraiture has, compared with the Viennese humanist portraits discussed earlier, undergone a fairly spontaneous and far-reaching transformation. Even in the earliest Wittenberg portraits the profoundly mysterious background has gone. The subjects of the portraits stand, very self-aware, in front of a neutral, luminous blue, green or grey expanse which gives them a grave, rather sober objectivity. It seems at first that Cranach is returning to a very outmoded conception of the portrait – to the days before it was capable of presenting the subject in his own distinctive setting and in a warm intimacy. But it soon becomes clear that Cranach's portraits can in no way be mistaken for those of the late German Gothic. The air of good breeding, the coolly superior mode of presentation, the objectivity everywhere apparent – in an artist usually so naïvely communicative and affable – are enough to prevent this. Rather is it obvious that these portraits are essentially related to the reserved portraiture of Hans Holbein the Younger. Realistic details and intimate shades of expression are increasingly renounced in favour of the universally valid and typical, form and expression are subjected to a stylisation of stringent and drastic economy. The phenomenon of this portraiture can be described but eludes analysis. Since Cranach's work is undoubtedly always based on 'modelli' drawn or painted from life the spontaneity of these first lifelike impressions still informs these compositions, which often have a fascinating off-centre arrangement. But the fleeting impression has been seized and held in a concentration of brilliant energy. This applies equally to the draughtsmanship, which is full of verve and originality. The sometimes remarkably Oriental 'line' becomes more and more the basic element in Cranach's portrait painting. The modelling of light and shadows is also concentrated along vibrant lines of ornamental charm and character so that head and body seem to be almost flat against the featureless expanse of background. Cranach, who in his early works employed light and shade with all the prodigality of a painter, tends increasingly towards a uniformly light, unbroken localised colouring, the ingenious art of the illuminator.

Cranach's search for a concentrated live formula occasionally transforms human faces into impressive masks which, though bordering on caricature, leave no doubt as to the 'resemblance' which is singled out for mention by contemporary witnesses. (See Plates 10, 11, 14–17, 19, 24–27, and I.)

Cranach's models are seldom particularly attractive: dumpy men, some gross and stupid, others moronic and deformed; strutting patricians; amiable if rather foolish-looking princes; rachitic princesses; ugly little princes. But there are also figures of calm distinction, loftily aristocratic or profoundly intellectual. There is no lack of charming, fashionable girls and women, no lack of refinement or coquetry. Great, pure beauty is rare. This slightly dubious, sometimes insecure quality often gives Cranach's portraits a most fascinating though indefinable interest. Cranach does not paint naïvely attractive, devout Gothic figures but men and women fully aware of their troubled times and reacting towards them not with a questioning revolt but with a stoical or epicurean charm.

There is one many-sided *genre* which has its legitimate place in the humanist and very life-loving atmosphere of the princely courts at the beginning of the sixteenth century, namely the erotic, to which category belong the numerous more or less voluptuous single nudes together with the 'ill-assorted couples' particularly popular in Cranach's workshop and also the 'scenes from antiquity'. The first, so far as is known, is Cranach's grandiose nude composition *Venus and Cupid*, 1509, in Leningrad. Life-size nudes are familiar to us from Dürer and Baldung Grien, but Cranach's nudes stand out at once because of their greater degree of voluptuous sensuality, of alluring, dreamy softness and they reveal clearly their courtly, lascivious, in fact decadent, character. Cranach, the popular and successful painter, knew very well how to cater for his patrons' tastes in this respect too. He does so with an instinctive certainty of the charms of the modish – closely resembling in this Renoir, who came three hundred years later. (See Plates 36, 37, 45.)

The flowing line of these more and more charming nudes is harmonious but bizarre. Cranach outlines the shape of the body with a sinuous line of hairbreadth accuracy and then dispenses with any further interior drawing or modelling. Form, attitude and gesture assume as a result a catlike softness, a certain feline charm. These very young girls have long legs and delicate limbs; they are slender to the point of leanness with small breasts and no full curves except their protruding stomachs. In fascinating contrast to these delicate bodies are the round peasant faces with the characteristic Slav touch: the prominent cheekbones and the narrow, slanting eyes. Somehow one is always reminded of mannequins displaying lingerie. Some five years after the Leningrad Venus comes Cranach's first *Judgment of Paris* – a subject he was repeatedly given. Then followed the naiads at rest in the attitude of Giorgione's Dresden *Venus*, the Lucretia scenes and similar works. Allied to these profane nudes and scarcely separable from them are the countless studies of Adam and Eve, now in two pictures, now together in one. The single figures become groups; the Three Graces, Caritas with many children, Hercules with Antæus, Apollo and Diana. Finally whole bands of nudes with constantly repeated themes such as *The Family of Fauns, Bacchus with a Host of Children, The Golden Age* and the *Silver Age*, etc. This preoccupation with 'scenes from antiquity' was peculiar to the period and is not at all unusual. Cranach is known to have had an imperfect knowledge of Latin, but as a friend of many scholars he knew as much of mythology and history as the average educated man.

To this same group belong, finally, the scenes of 'ill-assorted couples' so often named in court accounts; compositions containing a few half-lengths and harking back to the Netherlandish atmosphere of Quentin Massys: *The Old Lecher, The Payment, Old Man and Young Woman* – these and similar brothel scenes are sometimes sheer comedy. Their underlying irony is reminiscent of Shakespeare or Hogarth without the latter's moralising pathos. Cranach neither complains nor seeks to educate – he shows himself full of good-humoured understanding. Still strikingly handsome even as an old man, Cranach was anything but a killjoy. His celebrated courtesy and jovial affability indicate a gay pleasure-loving man who denied himself none of life's delights. (See Plates 40, 42, 44.)

Cranach's religious painting – which in his case must include the portraits of famous churchmen – was about as extensive as his profane work. Significantly in the foreground is Cranach's activity in the service and spirit of the Old Church, whose most prominent representative in Germany at that time was one of Cranach's most important patrons: the Cardinal Albrecht von Hohenzollern, residing in splendour at Halle close by. At that time the most powerful among the German Princes, also Elector and incumbent of three bishoprics or archbishoprics (Magdeburg, Mainz and Halberstadt), he was at the same time one of the most ostentatious art patrons of his day. He had all the great names in German art working for him and for ten years had the greatest of all as court painter – Mathias Grünewald (at least from 1516 to 1525). When it is remembered that this prodigal prince was not only the embodiment of everything that Cranach's friend Luther opposed, but was the direct target of Luther's most bitter attacks, and that Tetzel's sale of indulgences, engineered by the Cardinal, was the proximate cause of the Reformation, then one may well be astonished at Cranach's activities. They are indeed difficult to defend on the grounds of the artist's or subordinate's political and religious non-involve-

Three pictures painted by Cranach for Cardinal Albrecht of Brandenburg. – Fig. 2–a. *Cardinal Albrecht of Brandenburg kneeling before the Crucified.* About 1524. Munich, Alte Pinakothek. – Fig. 2–b. *The Man of Sorrows on the Sepulchre between the Virgin and S. John.* 1524. Freiburg, Cathedral. – Fig. 2–c. *Hercules and Omphale.* 1535. Copenhagen, Royal Museum of Fine Arts

Fig. 3. *Christ on the Cross*. (From the Schottenstift in Vienna.) About 1500. Vienna, Kunsthistorisches Museum

Fig. 4. *Madonna*. About 1537. Innsbruck, Parish Church

Fig. 5. *Martin Luther as S. George*. About 1521. Weimar, Schlossmuseum

ment. Instead we must realize that in the early days of the Reformation there was not that clearcut and irrevocable cleavage between the parties that developed later. Neither Luther himself nor Frederick the Wise were fully aware of their radical break with the Old Church because at first they abhorred and opposed only its temporary evils. In addition an authority like Cranach might claim for himself the sovereign freedom of choice. Cranach's workshop was an economic factor and, as is completely familiar to us in modern economic life, stood outside normal responsibility. When Cranach decided to support the Reformer and his cause he was giving this help from his own position of strength, but that did not necessarily imply any exclusive obligation.

Cranach's work for the Cardinal seems to have begun in 1520 and to have lasted until 1527. Between these two dates lies the brilliant period of Albrecht von Hohenzollern. In the previous year Grünewald had left the service of the Cardinal's court to be replaced by the painter later known as Pseudogrüne-wald, obviously the pupil of Cranach's mentioned earlier, Simon Franck. (Other pupils had already worked in the Cardinal's service.) No artist painted so many pictures of the Cardinal as Lucas Cranach the Elder. He painted the vain, pomp-loving Prince of the Church in half-length (examples in Berlin, Mainz, Leningrad, also the engraving of 1520). Then Albrecht sat for his portrait disguised as St. Erasmus, whom he had chosen as a patron of his 'New Foundation' in Halle, intended to act as a Catholic bulwark against Lutheranism, a 'Defence of Wittenberg'. At least twice Cranach portrayed the Cardinal as S. Jerome against an open landscape, and again twice 'in his Study' which owes something to Dürer's engraving *Jerome in his Study* of 1514. These pictures are dated 1525, 1526 and 1527 (see Plates 21 and 23). The most splendid portrait of Albrecht ever painted by Lucas Cranach is the picture in the Pinakothek in Munich (fig. 2–a), showing the Cardinal kneeling at prayer at the foot of the Cross in the attitude of a donor; this is one of Cranach's most expressive works. As in Cranach's earlier pictures landscape and figures are held together by a unifying, all-pervasive atmosphere. Above a mountainous landscape dark clouds presage a gathering storm. The heavy red of the Cardinal's robe combines with the dark tones of the landscape and the sky to form a sombre harmony of great dramatic force. The number of altarpieces painted for the Cardinal is difficult to determine. Some carry his armorial bearings, e.g. the masterly *Man of Sorrows between the Virgin and St. John* of 1524 in Freiburg (fig. 2-b). But most of the work carried out in Cranach's style for Albrecht must be from the hand of Cranach's pupil Simon Franck; other works, like the great *Resurrection and Ascension* in the Stifts-kirche at Aschaffenburg (1538) are directly and closely connected with Cranach's workshop, though their basic conception excludes the possibility of Cranach himself as their painter.

This most worldly churchman also commissioned Cranach to paint 'scenes from antiquity' which rivalled the erotic 'couples': *Hercules and Omphale*, 1535 (in Copenhagen), again bears the Cardinal's coat of arms (fig. 2-c).

The first altar-paintings Cranach produced after he was summoned to Wittenberg in pre-Lutheran days were already sharply differentiated from the *Crucifixions* and the *Rest on the Flight* of the Vienna period. Only in the Dresden *S. Catherine's Altar* and the Torgau *Altar* (cf. fig. 1 and Plate 9) may there still be seen landscape backgrounds in the 'romantic' style. Everywhere else a notable calm, even a gracious withdrawal, is apparent, matched by an increasingly smooth, firm and therefore more im-personal, official and cool style of painting. Pictures containing many figures, in the management of which Cranach is not very adept and which do not suit his talent at all, are sometimes mere amorphous crowds. Above all, that same Cranach who in his early days in Vienna had created the most gripping, turbulent pictures of the Passion now fails when attempting dramatic Passion scenes. It is clear that the courtier has to keep his feelings under tighter control: now that he is growing older and more mature, Cranach likes to husband his powers, to hold them in reserve for the expression of beauty, which now seems more important than anything else. The great portrait-painter has most success, as one would expect, with half-length religious subjects, especially with the countless serene yet ardent Madonnas who usually resemble each other but are never literal copies. The magical charm of Cranach's Madonnas never failed of its effect. These pictures had all the qualities needed to endear them to the common people. One Cranach Madonna, the so-called *Mariahilfbild* in the parish church at Innsbruck (fig. 4), inspired amateur painting for centuries: men never grew weary of repeating this lovely group on glass and on panels in Bavaria, Bohemia and Austria.

Cranach comes still closer to the people as a painter for the Reformation, a cause he served while working for Luther's arch-enemy, Cardinal Albrecht of Brandenburg. When Luther nailed up his theses in 1517, thus ushering in the Reformation, it was in this same town of Wittenberg, where Lucas Cranach the Elder was one of the leading spirits, nearly all of whom made common cause with the Reformer. Service of a cause usually implied for Cranach friendship with its leader. As with his princely patrons, so with Luther he formed close ties of sincere friendship. First the painter had been Luther's protector, then he became his confidant and finally his friend and admirer. We learn from an anecdote of an argument between Cranach and the Catholic Duke of Saxony in Dresden that the artist had Luther's name on his lips at every possible opportunity.

Cranach's earliest, at first modest, work for the Reformer dates from a year after the nailing up of the theses. Then in 1520 came the first portraits of Luther (repeated in variants), the engraving with the frontal-facing bust, followed the next year by the masterpiece with the lapidary head in profile, also an engraving. In 1520 Luther attended the christening of Cranach's daughter Anna as godfather. In 1521, after the Reichstag diet at Worms, Cranach was the first Wittenberger taken into Luther's confidence when he sought the protection of the Wartburg. Under the assumed name of George and disguised as a knight, the Reformer later returned to Wittenberg for three days. While there he took the opportunity of having Cranach paint his portrait.

This year and the following year Cranach provided the woodcut illustrations for a few reformational polemical writings and sold Lutheran publications in his bookshop, in particular the German translation of the New Testament. In 1525 Cranach, together with Bugenhagen and Apel, supported his friend (and recanting monk) in his wooing of Katharina von Bora, a runaway nun; they were bold, unprejudiced men with a taste for adventure, in whose company, strangely enough, the prosperous citizen, merchant and artist Cranach felt completely in his element. In 1526 the painter stood godfather to Luther's first son Johannes. In 1527 the Reformer's parents were staying in Wittenberg on a visit and had their portraits painted by Cranach. There is a completed version of these portraits in the Wartburg; Cranach's own brilliant study for the expressively ugly head of the father is now in the Albertina in Vienna (Plate 25). Here too Cranach obviously intended to repeat it as a panel painting.

Cranach frequented all the leading Reformers in Wittenberg. Philipp Melanchthon seems to have held his artistic gifts in particular esteem, naming him in the same breath as Dürer and Grünewald in an often-cited passage of 1532 and endeavouring to develop together with Cranach the idea of the Protestant picture. Melanchthon, in a letter to the poet Johann Stigel in 1544, tells how he had often placed at Cranach's disposal for him to develop completed drafts for dogmatic pictures in the new spirit. Luther on the other hand, hardly a connoisseur of art, seems to have had a fairly low opinion of Cranach's painting. In 1545 he remarked ironically ' . . . but Master Lucas is a crude painter. He could have been less hard on the female sex both because they are God's creatures and because they are our mothers. He should at the same time have painted the Pope in more worthy, I mean more devilish, guise.'

The human sympathy between the two men sprang from a totally different source. In 1537, when Cranach and his wife learned of the death of their son Hans in Bologna, Luther spoke wonderful words of consolation to the bereaved parents, which have been preserved in his table-talk. (If we are to believe the evidence of Stigel, Hans Cranach had dedicated himself with particular zeal to painting the Reformers' portraits; Luther alone he portrayed 'hundreds of times'.)

Later Cranach the Elder is said to have decorated a room in his house in the genuine Renaissance manner. Instead of the customary, often unconnected *uomini famosi* he painted in each of nine panels the great representatives of the new doctrine in his immediate circle, of whom Cranach was proud to count himself one: Luther, Melanchthon, Jonas, Bugenhagen, Cruciger, Forster, etc. In 1547, after Luther's death, Cranach's workshop completed the great Reformation altar in the parish church of Wittenberg, in which figure Luther, Melanchthon and Bugenhagen. The altar in Weimar parish church imposed a similar task on Cranach the Younger in 1555. In this so-called allegory of salvation Lucas Cranach the Elder himself appears in the immediate foreground together with Luther, as in many other paintings.

Cranach's essential contribution to the culture of the Reformation and to Protestant art, which is said to begin with him, are no doubt the countless portraits of the Reformers, and nothing else. Like Cranach's royal portraits, they developed into types of monumental significance. The image of the Reformers as painted by Cranach passed into the popular consciousness. We know them through Cranach (and many others who imitated or copied his portraits of Luther). They are detached representations treated in a broadly schematic manner: simple, impressive pictorial formulae for authorities on spiritual matters. But what of those didactic religious allegories (obviously of the greatest importance to the Reformers) for which Melanchthon provided the painter with the main outlines? If Cranach's work is studied in sufficient breadth from this point of view the yield would seem rather slender. There are here few themes that can be claimed as specifically Protestant, rarely any scenes which would not be equally well at home in the Old Church. *Luther preaching on the Crucifixion*, in the predella of the altar in Wittenburg parish church (mainly by Cranach the Younger), is not an Evangelical devotional work but at best a realistic illustration. The same is true of *Melanchthon administering baptism* and of *Bugenhagen hearing confession* and of a didactic representation of the Ten Commandments. In the *Luther working in the Vineyard of the Lord*, the illustration is turned into a kind of historical allegory. All these, however, are merely portraits of Reformers in action or means of visual instruction.

There is clearly one primary central Protestant theme: 'The Fall and the Salvation' or rather 'The Law and the Gospel'. This was treated often, in paintings, drawings and woodcuts, by Cranach himself, in his workshop, by his pupils, imitators and followers. The composition – whether divided in two halves by a tree or combined into a single whole – is always similar; one gets the impression that it may be based on an idea of Luther's, perhaps on a sketch by Melanchthon. On one and the same picture appear Adam and Eve, the soul of man banished from Paradise, Moses and the prophets, death and the devil, Christ as Judge of the world; then John the Baptist, Christ Crucified, the Lamb, the Dove, the brazen Serpent, the Risen Christ, the Annunciation to the Shepherds. And yet the idea of salvation embodied in this way is for the painter nothing more than a confused mass of persons, symbols and incidents of conflicting form and content with no visual link and with no clear and direct presentation of the intended basic idea – salvation of the sinner only by belief and grace.

It must be confessed that the Reformation had obviously less to offer its painters in the place of the subjects commissioned by the Old Church and of which its scorn of images and its iconoclasm deprived them. Luther and those of his immediate entourage were certainly not radical iconoclasts. They allowed pictures their due place 'provided you did not pray to them'. The Reformer argued that pictures, verses and hymns (and he himself provided models of the two latter often with moving endeavour, often with unconsciously magnificent success) were far better, more convincing preachers for the broad unlettered mass of the people than learned pulpit orators. The Reformers' mistake was to expect their artists to represent in pictures those abstract dogmas that were not good pictorial material as understood and loved by the Renaissance. In fact despite its good will Protestantism did lasting and subtle harm to the art of painting. Cranach, through his portraits of the Reformers, is the chronicler of the Reformation but not the founder of a genuine Protestant art.

Cranach's contemporaries singled out for mention three things in Cranach's painting: his closeness to nature, the speed with which the '*pictor celerrimus*' worked and the indefatigable industry he showed right into old age. The 16th, 17th and 18th centuries never tired of singing Cranach's praises. Not until towards the end of the last century was Cranach's art examined with a somewhat keener critical sense. Since about 1900 people have particularly preferred the early Cranach, rating his early work far above his maturer productions. But in the 1930's interest was especially directed towards those of Cranach's later works in which he strove less for expressive or representational values than for a tautly disciplined ('absolute') 'style' largely independent of them. And that is the present attitude of international criticism towards the master, the passionate stylist whose paramount insistence on form spans the centuries to join hands with the art of today.

NOTES ON THE REPRODUCTIONS IN THE TEXT

COLOUR PLATES

I. PORTRAIT OF LUCAS CRANACH AT THE AGE OF SEVENTY-SEVEN YEARS. Wood, 67×49 cm. Signed: snake with drooping bird's wings. Top right the inscription AETATIS SUAE LXXVII. 1550. Florence, Uffizi. (F–R 342.)
According to Friedländer (F–R, pp. 26 and 92) this portrait of the aged Cranach has 'a certain claim to be considered as by his hand because it was painted during the year (1550) which Cranach spent in Augsburg with his patron (Duke Johann Friedrich), presumably without assistants'. There is a very similar turn of the head, though facing the other way, in a few pictures that can with certainty be attributed to Cranach the Younger or his workshop: The *Allegory of Salvation* in Weimar Parish Church of 1555, the *Balthasar-Hofmann memorial* in the Leipzig Museum, the *Triptych* in Kemberg Parish Church. In this portrait there is no trace of that graphic stylization so characteristic of Cranach the Elder; whereas it possesses all the smoothness of surface typical of the style of Cranach the Younger. The facial structure has the indeterminacy, the mimic expression has the refined, rather flabby softness, occasionally found in Cranach the Younger, never the Elder. Finally, when the 'self-portrait' is compared with the artistically closely related *Portrait of an Unknown Man* in the Museum of Fine Arts at Breslau (F–R 344) hardly a doubt remains that the picture in Florence is not a self-portrait by Lucas Cranach the Elder but a portrait of him from the hand of Cranach the Younger. There was presumably a study in body colour for this portrait in the style of the Reims Studies for Heads (see Introduction p. 13) which was in fact made by Cranach the Elder himself, for there is no ground for assuming that the Uffizi portrait served as a model for the Cranach heads of the pictures in Weimar Parish Church and the Leipzig Museum. It is more likely that they are all based on the same original which has since been lost. (On Cranach's 'Self-Portraits' see J. Rosenberg, *Jahrbuch der Preussischen Kunstsammlungen*, 1932, pp. 204 f., and W. Scheidig in *Lucas Cranach, der Künstler und seine Zeit*, Berlin, 1953, pp. 129 f.)

II. THE HOLY KINSHIP (centre panel of the so-called Torgau Altar-piece). Wood, 120×99 cm. Signed: Lucas Chronus/Faciebat/Anno 1509. Frankfurt, Staedel Institute. (F–R 18.) (Detail from this picture: Plate 10.)
The centre panel shows in the left foreground two children, in the middle Joseph, Mary and S. Anne with the infant Christ and, on the balcony, S. Anne's three husbands, Joachim, Cleopas and Salomas. [Not reproduced here are: the left wing with Mary Cleopas and Alphaeus and their two children; the right wing with Mary Salome and Zebedee and their two sons S. John the Evangelist and S. James the Elder; and the outsides of the wings, painted in grisaille, so as to look like statues, with the Madonna and S. Anne. The panel in S. Mary's Church at Torgau, depicting the 'Auxiliary Saints', probably served as predella (F–R 15).]
Various portraits have been worked into the picture: Alphaeus bears the features of Frederick the Wise, Zebedee those of John the Constant. Other heads in this triptych have often been taken as representing Cranach, the Emperor Maximilian I, Sixtus Oelhafen (see Plate 10), John's deceased wife Sophie von Mecklenburg, John Frederick as a child, and others; but these identifications must be treated with caution.
Friedländer surmises that the S. Anne or Kinship Altar-piece was presented to a Spanish grandee by the Elector Moritz towards the end of April 1547 when King Ferdinand was visiting the castle and town of Torgau with several other princes. The altar-piece has been missing from Torgau since that visit. (F–R, p. 32.) It was in Cadiz well over a century ago and was acquired for the Staedel Institute in 1906. It has already been observed that Cranach seems to have been influenced here by certain Netherlandish artists, in particular Quinten Massys and Jan Gossaert. Details of costume and the grisaille technique do in themselves indicate Netherlandish influences, and even more the subtle play of light and shade, especially in the centre panel. It is worth noting in this connexion that before he completed his Kinship Altar-piece, Cranach did in fact spend a few months in the Netherlands towards the end of 1508. He may then have seen, for example, Massys' Kinship picture (now in the Brussels Museum), before completion; it bears the same date as Cranach's work, 1509.

MONOCHROME REPRODUCTIONS

Fig. 1. THE HOLY KINSHIP. Wood, 89×71 cm. Signed: snake with raised bat's wings. Vienna, Academy of Fine Arts. (F–R 33.) Detail of this picture: Plate 1.
The connexion between this picture and the 'Torgau Princes Altar-piece' has already been discussed (above). A self-portrait of Cranach can be identified with greater certainty in this Viennese picture than in the 'Princes Altar-piece'; E. Schenk zu Schweinsberg (Belvedere, 1926, pp. 67 f.) recognized it in the figure of the younger bearded man at the far left (of the spectator); see also the description of the detail, Plate 1 (p. 83).
Just as the Kinship picture of the so-called Torgau Princes

Altar-piece possesses, as has been shown, a certain Nether-landish character, so the effect of the striking perspective in the Viennese version is more Italian or at least southern; one thinks in particular of Michael Pacher and of Mantegna's circle so that the question arises whether Cranach ever came in contact at that time with South Tyrolean or Upper Italian art. In any case this painting marks a milestone in Cranach's development. It is comparatively the 'coldest', most intellectual pictorial expression of his art hitherto: perhaps it takes its tone from the courtly atmosphere in which Cranach now moves.

Fig. 2. THREE PICTURES PAINTED BY CRANACH AND HIS WORKSHOP FOR CARDINAL ALBRECHT OF BRANDENBURG.

Fig. 2a. CARDINAL ALBRECHT OF BRANDENBURG KNEELING BEFORE THE CRUCIFIED. Wood, 158 × 112 cm. Munich, Alte Pinakothek. (F–R 155.)
Restoration, particularly of the robe, has rather damaged the painting. This type of representation is akin to con-temporary German and Netherlandish tomb sculpture. On memorial portraits (which were not always placed on the tomb), the deceased is also often seen kneeling in prayer before the Crucifix or the Madonna. The fact that this picture was painted during the Cardinal's lifetime does not invalidate such an interpretation: it is not uncommon with memorial portraits. This Munich picture even seems to be mentioned in the Cardinal's will of 1540 among the 'vier taffeln, die erste mit unserm Conterfact, so lang wir seyn', four panels, the first one with our portrait in full length. We assume that 'so lang wir sein', does mean 'full-length', and not 'life-size'. The picture was removed from the Stiftskirche at Aschaffenburg in 1829 and sold to the State of Bavaria. It was to Aschaffenburg that the Cardinal had retired in 1541 from what had been his favourite place of residence, Halle an der Saale, to escape from the Refor-mation and from his creditors; he had taken with him almost all his movable art treasures. There is no doubt that the Munich picture was painted for Halle, where it hung either in the Moritzburg or in the Stiftskirche.
Cranach is known to have worked for the town of Halle and for the Cardinal between 1520 and 1526. During this period he created a whole series of portraits of the Prince, some of them dated.

Fig. 2b. THE MAN OF SORROWS ON THE SEPULCHRE BETWEEN THE VIRGIN AND S. JOHN. 1524. Wood, 108 × 84 cm. Signed: snake with upright wings. Freiburg, Cathedral. (F–R 733.)
It seems probable that this picture was also painted for Cardinal Albrecht and was intended to hang in Halle an der Saale, in view of the Prince's coat of arms on the back of the picture and the date 1524, for between 1523 and 1526 the Cardinal – so far as I am aware – commissioned works of art

exclusively for the castle (Moritzburg), the Stiftskirche (Cathedral) and the 'Neues Stift' in Halle.

Fig. 2c. HERCULES AND OMPHALE. 1535. Wood, 82 × 118 cm. Signed: snake with drooping wings. Copenhagen, Royal Museum of Fine Arts. (F–R 225.)
This picture with the surprisingly late date of 1535 also bears Cardinal Albrecht's coat of arms. The signature is also remarkable: a snake with drooping wings, which Cranach used regularly only after 1537. Friedländer (F–R, p. 70) thereby concludes that this is an early work by L. Cranach the Younger, which seems the more credible in that Lucas Cranach the Elder worked considerably earlier for the Cardinal, namely between 1520 and 1526.
Cranach and his workshop often repeated this theme with slight variations.

Fig. 3. CHRIST ON THE CROSS. Wood, 57 × 45 cm. Vienna, Kunsthistorisches Museum. (F–R 1.)
Identified as a work by Cranach by F. Dörnhöffer (*Jahrbuch der K.K. Zentralkommission*, N.F.II, 2, 1904, vol. 175 f.). This picture, formerly attributed to Lucas van Leyden, is today regarded as Cranach's earliest known work (see F–R, p. 27). This emotionally charged composition finds no echo in Cranach's other representations of the Crucifixion. Later Cranach relies more on Dürer for externals.

Fig. 4. MADONNA. Wood, 78.5 × 47.1 cm. Innsbruck, Parish Church. (F–R 317.)
According to Friedländer (F–R, p. 88) this picture dating from the 30's is a 'present from the Elector Johann Georg of Saxony to Archduke Leopold V, whose son, Archduke Ferdinand Karl, presented it to the townspeople; first in Passau, then in Innsbruck Castle, then from 1650 in the Parish Church. This so-called *Mariahilfbild* is one of the most popular forms in the history of Northern art: in popular art, in religious and decorative lay-art, in glass painting, in votive pictures etc. from the 16th to the 19th centuries one constantly encounters in Austria and Bavaria this delightful composition, in which Friedländer sees a connexion with Raphael's *Tempi Madonna* (Munich). If one is to postulate a source of inspiration outside Germany it should rather be sought in North Italy – perhaps in Donatello's, Mantegna's or Bellini's circle.

Fig. 5. *Martin Luther as S. George*. Wood, 51.5 × 33.5 cm. Weimar, Schlossmuseum. (F–R 126.)
There are several versions of this portrait of Luther. It is probable that all the variants go back to one and the same original study drawn from life, which could only have been made in 1521, because from 4th to 10th December of that year Luther was absent from the Wartburg and stayed incognito at Wittenberg under the name of Junker Jörg.

PLATES

The reproductions were selected and arranged in chronological order
by Ludwig Goldscheider, London.

1. THE ARTIST WITH HIS FAMILY. About 1510–12. Detail from the 'Holy Kinship' (Fig. 1). Vienna, Academy of Fine Arts

2. S. FRANCIS RECEIVING THE STIGMATA. About 1502. Vienna, Academy of Fine Arts

3. S. JEROME IN PENITENCE. 1502. Vienna, Kunsthistorisches Museum

4. Dr. Johannes Cuspinian. About 1502–3. Winterthur, Dr. Oskar Reinhart

ANNA CUSPINIAN. About 1502–3. Winterthur, Dr. Oskar Reinhart

6. CHRIST ON THE CROSS. 1503. Munich, Alte Pinakothek

7. THE REST ON THE FLIGHT INTO EGYPT. 1504. Berlin-Dahlem, Museum

8. Trees. Detail from Plate 6

9. SS. DOROTHEA, AGNES AND KUNIGUNDE. 1506. Right wing of the S. Catherine
Altar-piece, Dresden, Gallery

10. Emperor Maximilian and Sixtus Oelhafen (?). 1509. Detail from the so-called Torgau Altar-piece (Plate II). Frankfurt, Städel Institute

11. Duke Henry the Pious and his Wife. 1514. Dresden, Gallery

12. VIRGIN AND CHILD WITH S. ANNE. Munich, Alte Pinakothek

13. THE NATIVITY. Dresden, Gallery

14. SUPPOSED PORTRAIT OF A BURGOMASTER OF WEISSENFELS. 1515. Berlin-Dahlem, Museum

15. PORTRAIT OF A YOUNG GIRL. Paris, Louvre

16. 'A PRINCE OF SAXONY'. Washington, National Gallery of Art, Ralph and Mary Booth Collection

7. 'A PRINCESS OF SAXONY'. Washington, National Gallery of Art, Ralph and Mary Booth Collection

18. JUDITH. San Francisco, California Palace of the Legion of Honor

19. PRINCESS SIBYLLE OF CLEVE AS BRIDE. 1526. Weimar, Schlossmuseum

21. CARDINAL ALBRECHT OF BRANDENBURG AS S. JEROME IN HIS STUDY. 1526. Sarasota, John and Mable Ringling Museum

22. ADAM AND EVE. 1526. London, Courtauld Institute Galleries

23. Cardinal Albrecht of Brandenburg as S. Jerome in a Landscape. 1527. Berlin-Dahlem, Museum

24. Johannes Geiler von Kaisersberg. Munich, Alte Pinakothek

25. LUTHER'S FATHER. Tempera on paper. About 1527. Vienna, Albertina

26. PORTRAIT OF A YOUNG LADY. Copenhagen, Royal Museum of Fine Arts

27. PORTRAIT OF A SCHOLAR. 1529. Brussels, Museum

28. The Stag Hunt of the Elector Frederick the Wise. 1529. Vienna, Kunsthistorisches Museum

29. The Elector Frederick the Wise and Emperor Maximilian. Detail from Plate 28

30. THE DESTRUCTION OF PHARAOH. 1530. Regensburg, Staatsgalerie

31. Adam and Eve in the Garden of Eden. 1530. Vienna, Kunsthistorisches Museum

32. Diana and Actaeon. Hartford, Conn., Wadsworth Atheneum

33. Reclining Nymph. Lugano-Castagnola, Baron Thyssen-Bornemisza

FONTIS NYMPHA SACRI SOMNVM NE RVMPE QVIESCO.

35. Apollo and Diana in a wooded Landscape. 1530. Berlin-Dahlem, Museum

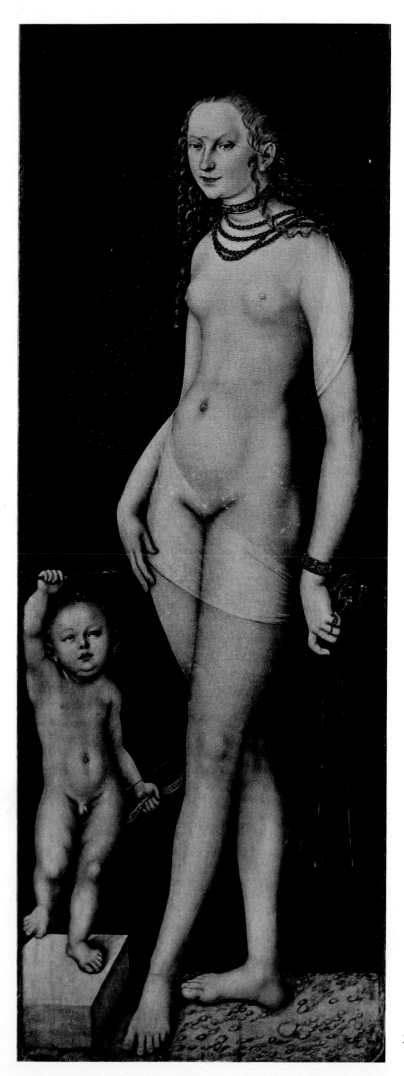

36. VENUS AND CUPID. Berlin-Dahlem, Museum

37. THE JUDGEMENT OF PARIS. 1530. Karlsruhe, Kunsthalle

38. THE FEAST OF HEROD. 1531. Hartford, Conn., Wadsworth Atheneum

39. THREE YOUNG LADIES. Vienna, Kunsthistorisches Museum

40. THE OLD LOVER. 1537. Vienna, Academy of Fine Arts

41. JUDITH. Stuttgart, Gallery

42. The Payment. 1532. Stockholm, National Museum

43. MELANCHOLY. 1532. Copenhagen, Royal Museum of Fine Arts

44. THE OLD LOVER. Besançon, Museum

46. THE FOUNTAIN OF YOUTH. 1546. Berlin-Dahlem, Museum

47. ARRIVAL OF THE OLD WOMEN. Detail from Plate 46

48. BIRDS. Tempera on paper. Dresden, Gallery

NOTES ON THE PLATES

In the TEXT two of Cranach's paintings are reproduced in colour
and referred to as Plates I and II.
The black and white reproductions in the TEXT are referred to
as Figs. 1 to 4.
The reproductions in the COLOUR PLATES SECTION
are referred to as Plates 1 to 48.

Abbreviations of the two works most often quoted:

F–R = M. J. Friedländer and J. Rosenberg, *Die Gemälde von Lucas Cranach*. Berlin 1932.
Rosenberg = Jakob Rosenberg, *Die Zeichnungen von Lucas Cranach dem Älteren*. Berlin 1960.

NOTES ON THE COLOUR PLATE SECTION

1. THE ARTIST WITH HIS FAMILY. Detail from *The Holy Kinship* (Fig. 1). Vienna, Academy of Fine Arts.
As has already been stated on p. 29 we may, with E. Schenk zu Schweinsberg (*Belvedere*, 1926, pp. 67 f.), see in the male figure on the extreme left a self-portrait of Cranach. Thus the woman seated before him on the ground is Barbara Brengbier, whom the artist had married in 1504 (seen here as Mary Cleopas). The woman seated on the ground at the right and the man at the extreme right would then be Cranach's parents-in-law (seen here as Zebedee and Mary Salome). Barbara's father was Town Councillor and Mayor of Gotha. The young woman, who would thus be a portrait of Cranach's wife, reappears in the *Expulsion of the Money-Changers* in Dresden.

2. S. FRANCIS RECEIVING THE STIGMATA. Wood, 86.8×47.5 cm. (slightly cut at the top). Vienna, Academy of Fine Arts. (F–R 3.)
Probably forms a pendant to S. *Valentine with Donor* in the same museum. Both pictures are obviously parts of a larger altar-piece. The style of both these pictures is close to the S. *Jerome in Penitence* in the Kunsthistorisches Museum in Vienna (Plate 3) and the *Christ on the Cross* in the Alte Pinakothek at Munich (Plate 6), dated 1502 and 1503.

3. S. JEROME IN PENITENCE. Wood, 55.5×41.5 cm. Dated below in the middle, 1502. Vienna, Kunsthistorisches Museum. (F–R 4.)
Cranach's earliest dated picture and, as far as we know the development of his style, one of his earliest now extant. According to Baldass, this picture may have been painted for Johannes Cuspinian and his first wife (*Jahrbuch der Preussischen Kunstsammlungen*, 1928, p. 76 f.); the owl and the parrot in the tree at the extreme left also occur in the Cuspinian portraits, Plates 4 and 5.

4. DR. JOHANNES CUSPINIAN. Wood, 59×45 cm. Cuspinian's coat of arms at the back. Winterthur, Dr. Oskar Reinhart. (F–R 6.)

5. ANNA CUSPINIAN, née Putsch. Wood, 59×45 cm. Winterthur, Dr. Oskar Reinhart. (F–R 7.)
These two portraits formed a diptych: the wedding, presumably the occasion for the painting, took place in Vienna at the turn of the year 1502/3. Cuspinian (really Spiessheimer; 1473–1529) was a lecturer in history at Vienna University and also held office as an Imperial Councillor. He was repeatedly portrayed as a person of importance, among others by Bernhard Strigel (1520). Cranach appears to have been on fairly intimate terms with this respected scholar, for he undertook other commissions for him – very probably the S. *Jerome in Penitence* in Vienna (Plate 3).

6. CHRIST ON THE CROSS. Wood, 138×99 cm. Dated at the bottom in the middle: 1503. Munich, Alte Pinakothek. (F–R 5.)
This masterpiece from Cranach's early Austrian period is one of the artist's most expressive creations. From now on this profile view of the Crucified with its highly dramatic effect was used repeatedly by German artists, first by Mathis Grünewald (about 1515 – lost and only known from a copy in the Fürstenbergische Gemäldegalerie, Donaueschingen) and also in various engravings and paintings of the 'Danube School' grouped around Altdorfer and Wolf Huber. Here too the young Cranach reveals himself as an innovator of revolutionary boldness.

7. THE REST ON THE FLIGHT TO EGYPT. Wood, 69×51 cm. Signed: L.C. interlaced with the date: 1504 above, at a slant. Berlin-Dahlem, Museum. (F–R 10/11.)
Cranach's earliest signed picture. It used to belong to the well-known art critic Konrad Fiedler, who had it from Italy (Rome, Palazzo Sciarra).

8. TREES. Detail from Plate 6. Munich, Alte Pinakothek.

9. SS. DOROTHEA, AGNES AND KUNIGUNDE. Right wing of the S. Catherine Altar-piece. Wood, 126×67 cm. This centre picture is signed: L.C. (close together) and dated 1506. Dresden Gallery. (F–R 13.)
On the reverse side of these altar wings were probably the pictures of similar format portraying SS. Christina, Ottilia, Genevieve and Apollonia. (F–R16.) The wing reproduced here was until the last war in the collection of Baron Speck von Sternburg in Lützschena near Leipzig. Scholars have taken the saints and other figures represented on this altar-piece to be portraits but they have failed to reach unanimity in matters of detail. The only identifications conceded by Friedländer are of the dashing rider with the humanist Hans von Schwarzenberg and of the two riders above with Frederick the Wise and John the Constant – both in the centre panel, but it is possible, in fact probable, that the female saints on the wings are also likenesses. The cherub in front of S. Dorothea is holding a basket of flowers as the saint's attribute.

10. EMPEROR MAXIMILIAN I AND SIXTUS OELHAFEN (?). Detail from the so-called Torgau Altar-piece (Plate II). 1509. Frankfurt, Staedel Institute.
See notes on Plate II. The identification of the man with a chain (Cleopas) as the Emperor and of his interlocutor (Salomas) as Oelhafen is due to G. Swarzenski (*Münchner Jahrbuch* 1907, p. 49 f.). The detail is reproduced two-thirds the original size.

11. DUKE HENRY THE PIOUS AND HIS WIFE. Transferred from wood to canvas, each 184.5×82.5 cm. The portrait of the Duchess is signed: L – snake – C., with the date 1514 above. Dresden, Gallery. (F–R 53–54.)

Known to be in the Dresden collection as early as 1641. Cranach was in constant and fairly close touch with the Duke who resided in Freiberg in Saxony. He portrayed him several times, and also painted his wife and their two sons. Cranach also drew for the Duke sketches for the decoration of cannon. Finally, Cranach dedicated to the Duchess, obviously an ardent supporter of the Protestant cause, a drawing on his favourite Protestant theme, the *Allegory of Redemption*.

12. VIRGIN AND CHILD WITH S. ANNE. Wood, 61×40 cm. Munich, Alte Pinakothek. (F–R 59.)

From the Boisserée Collection. This picture has been variously dated. In my opinion it is technically closest to the *Madonna* in Glogau of 1518 (F–R 81) and to the *Christ on the Mount of Olives* in Dresden (F–R 83) which Friedländer puts between '1515 and 1520'. (F–R, p. 45.)

13. THE NATIVITY. Wood, 30×23 cm. Signed: snake with upright wings. Dresden, Gallery. (F–R 90.)

In this subject the artistic problem is the mastery of the nocturnal effect built up of powerful contrasts of light and shade. According to Friedländer's hypothesis, Cranach had almost simultaneously made a copy of Hieronymus Bosch's *Last Judgement* in Vienna (F–R 88, Berlin) in which the nocturnal element also preponderates. There is hardly any doubt that German artists drew their inspiration for such bold artistic ventures from the Netherlands; however, it is important to establish that Cranach's night pieces are among the earliest in German art, along with Altdorfer's *Nativity*, Berlin (about 1515), Hans Baldung Grien's High Altar of Freiburg Cathedral (1516) and Hans Holbein's Oberriedaltar in Freiburg Cathedral (about 1522).

14. SUPPOSED PORTRAIT OF A BURGOMASTER OF WEISSENFELS. Wood, transferred to canvas. 42×28 cm. Signed: snake with upright wings beneath the date 1515. Berlin-Dahlem, Museum. (F–R 56.)

The same model at about the same age is believed to be represented in the study for a portrait, *Head of a Clean-shaven Man* in the Berlin Print-Room (Rosenberg 73). The riddle of the half-concealed inscription on the gold breastplate has not so far been solved.

15. PORTRAIT OF A YOUNG GIRL. Wood, 39×25 cm. Paris, Louvre. (F–R 130.)

Erroneously regarded as Luther's daughter Magdalena (see F–R, page 55).

16–17. A PRINCE AND A PRINCESS OF SAXONY. Wood, each 43.6×34.5 cm. Washington, National Gallery of Art. (F–R 104.) From the Ralph and Mary Booth Collection, Detroit; since 1947 in the National Gallery, Washington.

According to Friedländer (p. 50) the subjects were presumably a Prince and a Princess of Saxony. Of the children of the electoral house of Saxony of the period 1516–18 (Friedländer's dating of these portraits) these could be the children of Duke George the Bearded: Prince Frederick (born 1504) and Princess Christine (born 1505). In my view Friedländer's dating may be too early.

18. JUDITH. Wood, 80×56 cm. Signed: snake with upright wings. San Francisco, Palace of the Legion of Honor. According to the Museum Handbook (1960 p. 24) 'A Lady of the Saxon Court as Judith'. A long list of representations of Judith is given by Friedländer. (F–R, pp. 65, 66 and 82.)

19. PRINCESS SIBYLLE OF CLEVE AS BRIDE. Wood, 55×37 cm. Signed: snake with upright wings, and the date 1526. Weimar, Schlossmuseum. (F–R 244.)

Pendant to the portrait of *John Frederick the Magnanimous of Saxony as Bridegroom* in the same museum. Sibylle (1512–54) is portrayed here at the age of fourteen. The engagement took place on 8 September, 1526, the marriage on 3 June 1527.

20. DAVID AND BATHSHEBA. Wood, 36×24 cm. Signed: snake with upright wings between the date 15—26. Berlin-Dahlem, Museum. (F–R 173.)

21. CARDINAL ALBRECHT OF BRANDENBURG AS S. JEROME IN HIS STUDY. Wood, 124.5×81.5 cm. Signed: snake with upright wings, dated 1526. (Reproduced before the recent cleaning.) Sarasota, John and Mable Ringling Museum of Art. (F–R 158.)

On Cranach's activity for Cardinal Albrecht of Hohenzollern and his portraits of Albrecht, see Notes on Figs. 2a–c, p. 30. A very similar but rather simpler version dated 1525 in the Darmstadt Museum. (F–R 157.) Friedländer (F–R, p. 59) rightly points out the close connexion between this composition and Dürer's engraving of the same subject (B 60) of 1510.

Here Cranach exploits to the full all his gifts as a naturalist, not only in the expressive suggestion of space but also in the care and understanding with which he depicts all kinds of animals, most of which are irrelevant to the central theme. For this he had a wealth of studies to draw on, some of which have been preserved (see Rosenberg, pp. 60–70). On the wall with a window hangs one of Cranach's characteristic Madonnas. The Cardinal was also portrayed twice by Cranach as *S. Jerome in a Landscape* (see notes to Fig. 2a, p. 30, and to Plate 23).

22. ADAM AND EVE. Wood, 117×80.5 cm. Signed: snake with upright wings, and dated 1526. London, Courtauld Institute Galleries (Lee Collection). (F–R 161.)

Of Cranach's numerous representations of the Fall of Man (see F–R, p. 99) the version in the Lee Collection is one of the richest and most attractive.

23. CARDINAL ALBRECHT OF BRANDENBURG AS S. JEROME IN A LANDSCAPE. Wood, 148×110 cm. Signed: snake with upright wings, and the date 1527 beneath. Berlin-Dahlem, Museum. (F–R 156.) See Notes on Fig. 2a and Plate 21.

24. JOHANNES GEILER VON KAISERSBERG. Wood, 30×23 cm. Munich, Alte Pinakothek. (F–R 249.)
Humanist and popular preacher in Strassburg Cathedral (1445–1510). Friedländer (F–R, p. 74) thinks that the portrait was probably painted from the woodcut portrait of Geiler on the title page of 'Doctor Keisersberg's Postill', Strassburg 1522. Another famous portrait of Geiler was painted from life in 1490 by Hans Burgkmair the Elder when only seventeen (Augsburg, Gallery; see E. Buchner, *Das deutsche Bildnis der Spätgotik und der frühen Dürerzeit*, Berlin, 1953, p. 92, Plate 93).

25. LUTHER'S FATHER. Tempera on paper, cut out and pasted on a new sheet of paper. 19.6 × 18.3 cm. Vienna, Albertina (Rosenberg 76).
Of all Cranach's portrait studies in tempera this one has the greatest claim to authenticity (whereas the others, particularly the whole Reims series (Rosenberg 77 f.) are generally attributed to Cranach the Younger).
Luther's parents appear to have visited Wittenberg in 1527 (see F–R, p. 75); on this occasion Cranach probably caught their likeness in preparatory sketches. Then Cranach used this study of Hans Luther for the painting now hanging in the Wartburg (F–R 253); it bears the date 1527. The corresponding study for the companion-piece, the portrait of Luther's mother, Margarethe, is missing.
There is no other of Cranach's studies for portraits which is so directly and perfectly linked with a finished painting as this one is with the picture in the Wartburg – an instructive testimony to the way Cranach used to employ his preparatory sketches in the final painted version.

26. PORTRAIT OF A YOUNG LADY. Wood, 40×25 cm. Signed: snake with upright wings. Copenhagen, Royal Museum of Fine Arts. (F–R 148.)

27. PORTRAIT OF A SCHOLAR. Wood, 51.5×39 cm. Signed: snake with upright wings, in between the date 15—29. Brussels, Museum. (F–R 266.)
An 18th-century inscription above: 'Johannes Scheuring Dr.' According to Friedländer this identification is certainly false (see F–R, p. 78) and the picture is far more likely to represent the mathematician, geographer and astronomer Dr. Johannes Schöner (1477–1547). Even this is uncertain. In any case we have here probably Cranach's most expressive, most starkly realistic portrait – possibly his greatest achievement as a portraitist.

28. THE STAG HUNT OF THE ELECTOR FREDERICK THE WISE. Wood, 80×114 cm. Signed: snake with upight wings; dated 1529. Vienna, Kunsthistorisches Museum. (F–R 231.)
In the foreground, as huntsmen, Emperor Maximilian I, Frederick the Wise and the Elector John the Constant. The two first named were already dead by the date of the picture, but not the Elector, who most probably commissioned it. There is no doubt that the workshop had a share in the execution. Cranach takes the opportunity of displaying to the full his celebrated gifts as a painter of animals.

29. THE ELECTOR FREDERICK THE WISE AND EMPEROR MAXIMILIAN. Vienna, Kunsthistorisches Museum. Detail from Plate 28. Both portraits are posthumous: Frederick had died in 1525, Maximilian as early as 1519.

30. THE DESTRUCTION OF PHARAOH. Wood, 82×117 cm. Signed: snake with upright wings, dated 1530. Regensburg, Staatsgalerie. (F–R 168.)
A very interesting composition, but one of Cranach's eccentric landscape paintings: compare it with his earlier romantic and naturalistic landscapes, particularly in Plates 4 and 7.

31. ADAM AND EVE IN THE GARDEN OF EDEN. Wood, 81 × 114 cm. Signed: snake with upright wings, dated 1530. Vienna, Kunsthistorisches Museum. (F–R 167.)
In the background from right to left: Creation of Adam, the Fall, Creation of Eve, Discovery of the Sinners, Expulsion from Paradise.

32. DIANA AND ACTEON. Wood, 50×73 cm. Signed: snake with upright wings. Hartford (Connecticut), Wadsworth Atheneum (Gallup Sumner and Mary Catlin Sumner Coll.).
Friedländer mentions three pictures on this subject. (F–R, p. 90.) The present version was in the hands of G. C. Beireis in Weimar; in 1928 it was exhibited by P. de Boer's in Amsterdam (Friedländer dated it on that occasion 'about 1525').

33. RECLINING NYMPH. Wood, 73×119 cm. Lugano-Castagnola, Baron Thyssen-Bornemisza. (F–R 101.)
On the possible Italian sources of inspiration see Introduction p. 10. Friedländer (F–R, p. 109) mentions no fewer than ten versions of this subject. The inscription common to nearly all: *Fontis nympha sacri somnum ne rumpe quiesco* means roughly: 'I, the nymph of the sacred spring, am resting here; do not disturb my sleep'.

34. JEALOUSY. Wood, 50.2×35.7 cm. London, National Gallery. (F–R 215.)
On the content of the picture see in particular Michael Levey *National Gallery Catalogues, the German School*, London, 1959, pp. 21 f. The subject has no doubt a slender connexion with Hesiod's description of the end of the Silver Age and is supposed to represent the effects of jealousy.

35. APOLLO AND DIANA IN A WOODED LANDSCAPE.
Wood, 51×36 cm. Signed: between the figures 15 and 30
the snake with upright wings. Berlin-Dahlem, Museum.
(F–R 222.)
Two variants are known, one of them in Buckingham
Palace.

36. VENUS AND CUPID. Wood, 172×63 cm. Berlin-
Dahlem, Museum. (F–R 199.)
On the probable Italian sources of inspiration see p. 10 of
the Introduction. Cranach treated this subject very fre-
quently.

37. THE JUDGEMENT OF PARIS. Wood, 35×24 cm.
Signed and dated: snake with upright wings and dated 1530.
Karlsruhe, Kunsthalle. (F–R 210.)
Several versions known.

38. THE FEAST OF HEROD. Wood, 80×117 cm. Signed:
snake with upright wings, dated 1531. Hartford (Conn.),
Wadsworth Atheneum. (F–R 182.)

39. THREE YOUNG LADIES. Wood, 62×89 cm. Vienna,
Kunsthistorisches Museum. (F–R 240.)
The fact that the half-length figure on the right is repeated
fairly closely in a Portrait of a Lady in the Uffizi (F–R 241) has
led scholars to assume that all three ladies in this Viennese
picture are portraits ('Three Sisters', see F–R, p. 73). Such
triple portraits on one picture are certainly rare and could
well be a further proof of Cranach's originality. But perhaps there is a mythological or allegorical meaning underlying this charming composition, which would then suggest
Italian models, particularly Venetian and Emilian.

40. THE OLD LOVER. Wood, 51×36.5 cm. Signed: snake
with upright wings, date 1537. Vienna, Academy of Fine
Arts. (F–R 232.)
Friedländer reads the date 1531. This half lascivious, half
moralising type of picture, which may derive ultimately
from the erotic literature of antiquity was suggested to
Cranach either by some Netherlandish pictures, such as the
one by Quinten Massys in the Louvre, or by Italian models,
such as the picture, dated 1503, Jacopo de' Barbari, in
Philadelphia, Johnson Collection (see Introduction pp. 10,
14, 19, 20). Cranach reversed the theme in The Payment,
in which an old woman is giving money to a youth
(example in the Budapest museum).

41. JUDITH. Wood, 86×59 cm. Signed: snake with upright wings. Stuttgart Gallery. (F–R 190.)

42. THE PAYMENT. Wood, 108×119 cm. Signed: snake
with upright wings, and dated 1532. Stockholm, National
Museum. (F–R 236.)
See notes on these 'Ill-assorted Couples' in the Introduction,
p. 20 and on Plate 40.
The particular charm of this extended version of one of
Cranach's favourite themes derives from the still-life on the
back wall and the table. The hanging game is reminiscent
of very similar animal studies in Dresden (Rosenberg 68–70;
see also Plate 48).

43. MELANCHOLY. Wood, 51×97 cm. Signed: snake
with upright wings and dated 1532. Copenhagen, Royal
Museum of Fine Arts. (F–R 227.)
There is a certain similarity between the principal figure of
this picture with the figure of Melancholia in Dürer's
engraving of 1514.

44. THE OLD LOVER. Wood transferred to canvas,
79×57 cm. Besançon, Museum.
Not very well preserved. Variant of the picture of about the
same dimensions in Nuremberg. (F–R 235.) Latest and most
impressive version of this theme, probably about 1532.

45. VENUS. Wood, 37×24 cm. Signed: snake with upright
wings and the date 1532. Frankfurt, Staedel Institute.
(F–R 204.)

46–47. THE FOUNTAIN OF YOUTH. Wood, 121×148 cm.
Signed: snake with bird's wings. Date 1546. Berlin-Dahlem,
Museum. (F–R 327.)
In Friedländer's view (F–R, p. 90) an authentic work by
the elder Cranach despite its late date of origin and the
altered signature 'because precisely from 1546 onwards his
son's style becomes more sharply differentiated'. This view
is certainly justified.

48. TWO BIRDS. Bodycolour on paper. 34.6×20.3 cm.
Dresden, Gallery. (Rosenberg 69.)
See notes on Plates 22, 28 and 42. Rosenberg (p. 27) dates the
work 'about 1530'.
The birds depicted here are called waxwings or chatterers
(ampelis garrula), in U.S.A.: cedarbirds or cedar-larks, or in
some districts, silk-tails. They are about 8 in. long.

INDEX OF COLLECTIONS

The publishers wish to thank the owners of private collections and the Directors of Museums for their kind permission to reproduce the Cranach paintings chosen for inclusion in this volume.